We Need PEOPLE POWER to Address a World In Peril

Hardy Merriman

**A Framing Essay for the
2023 Copenhagen People Power Conference**

We Need People Power to Address a World in Peril: A Framing Essay for the 2023 Copenhagen People Power Conference
By Hardy Merriman (2023)

This essay has been slightly modified from its original version.

Published by ICNC Press

This publication is part of the REACT (Research in Action) collaboration between ActionAid Denmark (AADK) and ICNC.

International Center on Nonviolent Conflict
600 New Hampshire Ave NW, Suite 1010
Washington, D.C. 20037 USA
www.nonviolent-conflict.org

SERIES EDITOR: Bruce Pearson
INTERIOR LAYOUT: Aaron Troia
CONTACT: icnc@nonviolent-conflict.org

Contents

Foreword

A recent United Nations report concluded that actors such as governments and civil society must embrace and enable social movements as essential partners in "building back better" from the intersecting crises of today.* The Copenhagen People Power Conference is a contribution to understanding how we can do this more effectively. We are bringing together movement leaders, as well as representatives of governments, parliaments, academia, the private sector, multilateral institutions, foundations, media, activists and civil society organizations from more than 60 countries around the world. We hope the discussions will produce new insights on how different actors can

---

* United Nations Human Rights Office of the High Commissioner, "Governments Must Embrace and Enable Social Movements As Key Partners in 'Building Back Better': UN Expert," news release, 28 October 2022, https://www.ohchr.org/en/press-releases/2022/10/governments-must-embrace-and-enable-social-movements-key-partners-building.

better support movements and start building the relationships that can make it happen.

To set the stage for our discussions we have invited Hardy Merriman from the International Center on Nonviolent Conflict to prepare this framing essay on the state of the social movements within three key themes we will be discussing at the conference. I hope the essay provides a strong basis for new dialogues and insights at the conference and in the coming years.

Welcome to Copenhagen!

Tim Whyte
Secretary General
Mellemfolkeligt Samvirke/ActionAid Denmark

Introduction

The world confronts three grave and interrelated crises.

Authoritarianism has been rising worldwide for nearly two decades. *Climate change* has been increasingly studied and publicly foretold since the 1970s.[1] Rising *violent conflict and insecurity* are a predictable result of autocratic waves and climate chaos.

The warning signs were clear for years. Many people tried to ensure that governments and multilateral institutions would take adequate preventative action to address these crises and protect humanity from their worst consequences. Civil society and policymakers invested extensively in institutional engagement and advocacy, built on the premise that data, reasoning, public education, and the public interest would galvanize a response proportionate to these challenges.

Decades of this work yielded positive effects,

but it has also been inadequate. Presently these crises have grown to existential proportions—democracies are backsliding; autocrats are coordinated, brazen, and powerful; atmospheric carbon is rising; and societal violence, conflict, and the risk of spreading war escalate.

The Necessity of People Power

There is no time to waste in responding more fully and effectively to these current trends (which some term a "polycrisis").[2] At stake are the freedom, peace, prosperity, stability, human rights, and livelihoods of present and future generations. Urgent and coordinated strategies are needed.

Top-down efforts of governments, multilateral institutions, and corporations continue to be necessary, but they have proven to be insufficient by themselves. Too frequently political and economic incentives pull their actions toward denial, delay, and incrementalism.

In the wake of institutional failure, communities organize people power movements and frequently use tactics of civil resistance—such as strikes, boycotts, civil disobedience, protests, noncooperation, and other nonviolent actions—to demand change. These movements educate, mobilize,

Definitions: Movements and People Power

In this paper, movements are defined as ongoing collective efforts to make consequential change in a social, economic, or political order. They are civilian-based, involve widespread popular participation, and alert, educate, serve, and mobilize people.[3]

Movements often emerge from the edges of formalized civil society and are frequently led by and initially composed of people who are directly affected by a particular problem. They involve both mobilization and organization—they are not spontaneous or disorganized outbursts. Movements may include formal organizations (sometimes these are referred to as "social movement organizations") but they are bigger than any one organization or coalition, because their essential aspect is voluntary participation from citizens (meant here as people who live in a certain place, rather than a particular legal status) and communities.

People power (also called "civil resistance" or "nonviolent action") is the use of a wide range of nonviolent tactics—such as strikes, boycotts, slowdowns, protests, civil disobedience, creation of alternative institutions, and many other acts of noncooperation—to achieve social, economic, or political change. Through these tactics (which often involve the exercise of internationally recognized human rights), people power shifts collective behavior in strategic and targeted ways in order to shift the balance of power in society. People power can also be effective at shifting societal narratives about legitimacy, fairness, equality, and relationships between groups in society.

While people power tactics are distinct from official institutional channels of making change (such as elections and the legal system), in practice many movements engage in both people power and institutional methods.

empower, forge alliances, and renew citizen participation. They also impose costs on abusers and advance solutions that can meet the magnitude and velocity of the threats that society faces.

A critical opportunity of the current moment is to achieve greater alignment of top-down approaches and bottom-up pressure. Movements need institutions in order to make policy change, but institutions need movements to hold them accountable and shift political and economic incentives so that meaningful policy change becomes possible. It is therefore through combined efforts that turning the tide on autocracy, climate change, and violent conflict can happen.

Yet proponents of top-down approaches and bottom-up movements have not always had harmonious relationships. Within institutions, misconceptions about movements persist, and engaging with movements can be complex. Answers to questions of *who* to engage with, *how*, and *when* are not always obvious. Movements also resist external control and may take actions that place institutional actors in dilemmas. Furthermore, institutional allies may fear that efforts to help movements could inadvertently backfire, potentially exposing movements to charges of being externally backed, or of being coopted.

These risks are not reasons for institutional allies to shy away from movement engagement—rather they are reasons to lean in. An established body of research tells us that people power movements have been one of the most powerful drivers of democracy worldwide over the past century.[4] These movements are also critical factors in producing better climate and peace and security outcomes.[5]

Moreover, research and past practice offer significant insight into how to work effectively with movements.[6] In short, the complexities of doing so are navigable.

In the following pages, the essential role of movements countering authoritarianism, climate change, and violent conflict are outlined, with commentary on how institutional allies can better enable and support them.

Countering Rising Authoritarianism

The Challenge

A powerful autocratic wave is sweeping the globe. According to various measures, the world is facing its seventeenth consecutive year of democratic decline, and the average global level of democracy has sunk to its lowest point since 1986.[7]

A more autocratic world is a world more dangerous for people everywhere—including those who currently live in democracies—as authoritarianism brings increasing risk of violent conflict, instability, and insecurity; humanitarian crises; corruption; undermining of multilateral institutions; harboring of violent non-state actors; and attacks on democracies.[8] Autocracies have also proven significantly less effective at fighting climate change.[9]

To ensure long-term peace, security, and human rights for populations around the world, it is therefore critically important that the current autocratic trend be reversed. But what will it take to foster a new democratic wave?

The Role of Movements

Three research findings offer a baseline for evaluating movements and their role in confronting authoritarian rule.

First, civil resistance has become the prevailing global means by which societies challenge autocrats. Research finds that the number of new movements with "maximalist goals" (creating a political transition, expelling a foreign occupier, or achieving territorial independence) has increased dramatically since the 1990s—with 42 new movements emerging between 1990–1999, compared to 96 new movements emerging between 2010–2019.[10] This rise is in part a result of the current autocratic wave. As governments become unaccountable, corrupted, and abusive under dictatorships and backsliding democracies, people lose confidence in institutional channels for making change and therefore seek alternative means of advancing their social, economic, and political goals. In addition to movements demanding democracy, large numbers of local and national nonviolent campaigns also pursue a range of related human rights, including the rights of women, minorities, and marginalized communities; labor rights; and transparency and the rule of law.

Second, civil resistance movements are critical in advancing democratic transitions. Between 1900 and 2019, civil resistance movements with maximalist aims achieved their goals 51 percent of the time, versus approximately a 26 percent success rate of violent insurgencies over this same timeframe.[11] In addition, once a transition against an autocrat occurs, ensuing prospects for democracy and other stabilizing factors have proven significantly higher for civil resistance-led transitions. For example, between 1900 and 2006, 57 percent of maximalist civil resistance movements were found to result in democratic outcomes five years after achieving a political transition.[12] In contrast, when a violent insurgency forced a political transition, it led to a democratic outcome only 6 percent of the time.[13] Civil resistance-driven transitions are also associated with rebounds in a country's life expectancy rate when compared to transitions driven by violent insurgency.[14]

Transitions spurred by civil resistance also significantly outperform elite-driven (top-down)

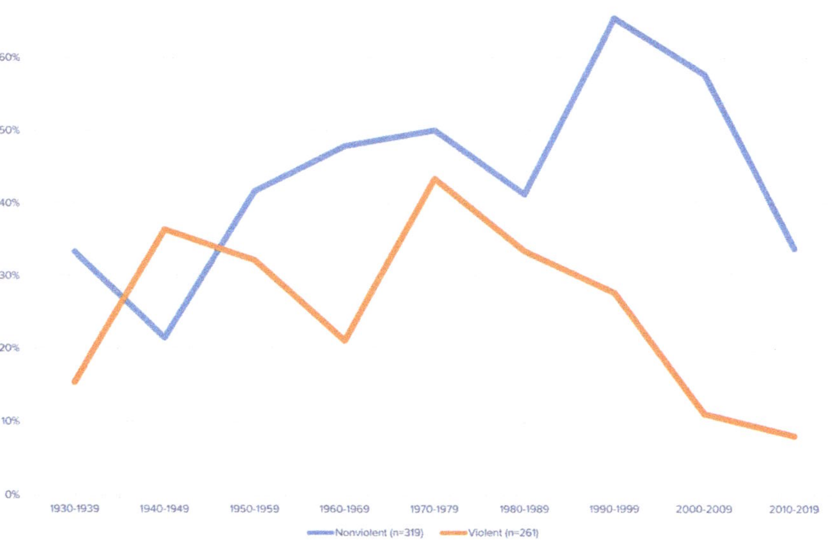

Source: Erica Chenoweth, "The Future of Nonviolent Resistance," in *Journal of Democracy* 31, no. 3 (July 2020).

transitions in producing durable democratic gains. Research finds that between 1972 and 2004, elite-led transitions that were unaccompanied by a popular nonviolent movement achieved a democratic outcome only 14 percent of the time.[15] Beyond this, civil resistance-driven transitions have been found to lead to greater economic growth than their top-down counterparts.[16]

Movements have further proven adept at protecting democracy when it is attacked, and play a powerful role in countering democratic backsliding.[17]

Third, civil resistance movement success rates have declined sharply in recent decades. The high water mark for movement success rates was 65 percent during the 1990s, but this declined to 34 percent in the 2010s, and fell further in the first few years of the present decade amidst the COVID-19 pandemic.[18]

Thus, at a time when autocracies are resurgent, the success rates of one of the most powerful democratic forces in the world is falling.

Ironically, this trend emerges from past success. Two decades ago, popular, nonviolent democratic transitions against authoritarian and corrupt rulers in Serbia (2000), Georgia (2003), and Ukraine

(2004) caught the attention of autocrats around the world. Subsequently, dictators and demagogues invested heavily in developing their skills, strategies, capacities, and transnational coordination to prevent and counter civil resistance movements. However, no comparable and comprehensive counter-investment took place among movement allies.

This issue demands urgent attention, as any viable strategy to reverse global authoritarianism will depend significantly on effective, bottom-up civic pressure. Fortunately, there are numerous actions that democratic governments, INGOs, philanthropies, diaspora groups, and others can take to support movements.

Opportunities and Potential Next Steps

The impacts of most forms of support to pro-democracy movements have been found to be context-dependent.[19] For example, in some cases economic sanctions against authoritarian governments have helped movements, and in other cases they have likely had a negative effect. Likewise, in some cases direct funding has helped movements, and in other cases it has been counterproductive. This leads to the first principle of movement support, which is to engage with and **listen closely to the needs of local actors. Any movement support should seek to respond to their needs and be an extension of (rather than a substitute for) their strategy.** It is through responsive engagement with local actors that support becomes more effective.

In addition, research generally suggests that **one of the most helpful forms of support to movements is through offering training for activists and organizers.** Notably, movements that receive training are associated "with high [levels of public] participation, low fatalities, and greater likelihood of defections" from their opponent's supporters.[20] This reflects the view that investing in a movement's skills and strategic choices can enable it to overcome challenging conditions, seize opportunities, and prevail over entrenched adversaries.

Heightened collaboration by movement allies is also critically important to increase efficacy.[21] Advocacy NGOs, philanthropies, governments, multilateral institutions, diaspora populations, and other entities each have specific comparative advantages in supporting democracy and human rights movements, and they are far more impactful when they coordinate their efforts.

Furthermore, as a movement evolves, its needs will change as well, and **developing support frameworks based on movement phases can also help a variety of external actors orient their activities.**[22] From the earliest stages of a movement, to times of peak mobilization, repression, transition, and post-transition, external actors should be prepared to offer both rapid and long-term forms of support, depending on a movement's circumstances.

There is much more that can be said on this topic, but one further point is that **democratic governments can take actions in their foreign policies to create an enabling environment for pro-democracy and human rights movements.**[23] By forming deeper alliances among fellow democracies, and recognizing the existential threat that growing authoritarianism presents, democracies must advance policies that counter authoritarianism, advocate for human rights, and support the protection of civil society. It is imperative that these strategic priorities be increasingly incorporated and given significant weight in international trade and security relationships.

Stopping Climate Chaos

The Challenge

Comprehensive impacts of climate change on humanity are now daily news. Unless more drastic and urgent action is taken in the next few years, these realities—ranging from food insecurity; humanitarian crises; storm and sea-level flooding, drought, extreme heat, and wildfires; animal and plant extinctions; spreading disease; economic disruptions; involuntary mass migration; increasing risk of violent conflict—threaten ultimately to end society as we know it. As UN Secretary-General António Guterres remarked on the March 2023 release of the Intergovernmental Panel on Climate Change (IPCC) report: "This report is a clarion call to massively fast-track climate efforts by every country and every sector and on every timeframe. In short, our world needs climate action on all fronts — everything, everywhere, all at once."[24]

Yet global CO_2 emissions from fossil fuel combustion reached an all-time high in 2022 and atmospheric carbon in 2023 continues to break new records.[25] Fossil fuel companies show no signs of self-restraint—in 2022, the "big five" (Exxon, Chevron, Shell, BP, and TotalEnergies) earned record profits of nearly US$200 billion, and more than US$1 trillion was invested globally in fossil fuel infrastructure and extraction.[26] Amidst these record profits, governments worldwide simultaneously continued to financially support gas, oil, and coal, even after many previously pledged to stop doing so. For example, G20 nations subsidized fossil fuels at a total of $1.4 trillion in 2022, of which $440 billion supported *new* investments in fossil fuel production.[27]

The evidence is clear: decades of dire warnings have been met with slow and inadequate responses, and a prime reason for this is that business interests have corrupted public institutions. With vast economic resources, fossil fuel, utility, agriculture, transportation, and related companies exert enormous leverage on political leaders and government and non-governmental sectors. They also foster misinformation and misdirection campaigns so that members of the public become confused, polarized, and ultimately fail to demand effective action from government and corporate officials.

The Role of Movements

The science explaining climate change has been apparent for decades. The knowledge and technologies exist to make a just transition to a carbon-neutral economy. The primary obstacle to responding effectively to the magnitude and scope of the crisis is a lack of political will.

Ordinary people are the largest untapped source of energy in this fight. Citizens in countries around the world are a vast reserve of power, and nonviolent action is the strategy that is open to all of them. People power has the capacity to rebalance relationships, impose costs, and create leverage so that multilateral dialogues are productive, government institutions fulfill their public mandates, and market forces drive investment in sustainable energy practices.

Numerous research findings suggest or conclude that public mobilization is impactful.[28] For example, a study evaluating protest activity and emissions levels in US states from 1990 to 2007 found that "the level of emissions in a state declines in states with increases in pro-environmental protest."[29]

This ability of environmental-based mobilization to affect government and industries is not just confined to democracies either. For example, environmental concerns and grievances have been at the heart of many popular protests in China, where they have led to government concessions and policy changes.[30]

Moreover, environmental activism has the proven ability to form a self-reinforcing cycle, creating an on-ramp for more citizens to get involved over time. Research suggests that climate marches can motivate bystanders to become engaged in activism.[31] Nonviolent tactics such as marches and civil disobedience have also been found to increase public support for climate movements, and thus the potential number of sympathizers from which those movements may recruit subsequently.[32]

Reflecting these and other findings, some philanthropy researchers argue that movements are one of the most cost-effective investments that can be made to stop climate change, with more carbon emissions averted per dollar/Euro given to movements than when given to more conventional environmental advocacy organizations.[33]

Opportunities and Potential Next Steps

Movements for climate justice face an unprecedented challenge. Stopping carbon emissions requires systems-level transformation across many aspects of society, including energy production and use, agriculture, transportation, manufacturing, urban and rural development, water consumption, finance, and trade policy.

Simultaneously, these aspects of society must be altered to enable a "just transition" that addresses inequities about who profits from, and who suffers from, past fossil fuel usage and the transition to a sustainable economy.

In this regard, climate justice puts carbon *and* human beings at the center of its policy goals.[34] It recognizes that the laws of physics require a non-negotiable transformation of fossil fuel economies, and this must be done in a way that is fair to people within societies as well as internationally.

Such a vast scope of change demands a broad-scale movement, and the diversity of geographies and issue areas relevant to climate justice offers many opportunities for allies to play supportive roles. The principles and practices (such as the benefits of supporting training, and heightened donor coordination) outlined in the previous

Graph 2. Global Atmospheric CO$_2$ Concentration, World

Atmospheric carbon dioxide (CO$_2$) concentration is measured in parts per million (ppm).

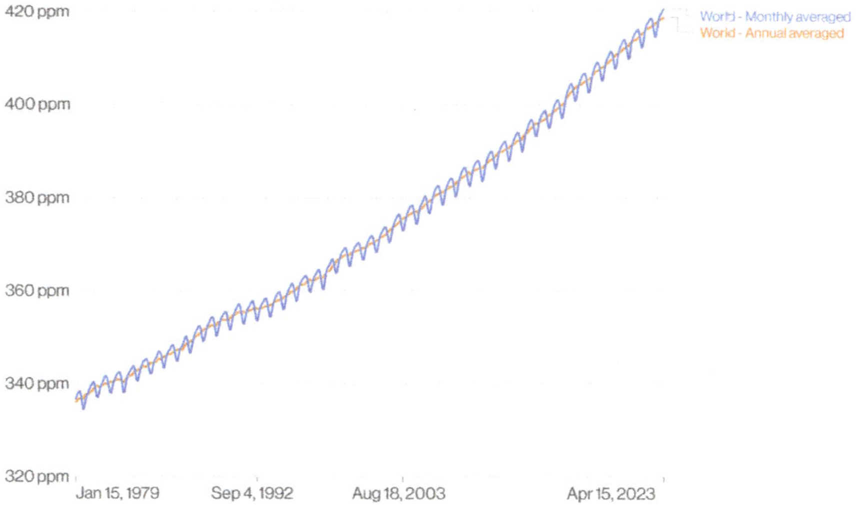

Source: National Oceanic and Atmospheric Administration (NOAA)

Source: Hannah Ritchie, Max Roser, and Pablo Rosado, "CO$_2$ and Greenhouse Gas Emissions," *Our World in Data*, May 2017. https://ourworldindata.org/co2-and-greenhouse-gas-emissions.

section on supporting democracy movements also apply to climate justice movements. Several further considerations are outlined below.

First, fostering movement coalitions and diverse linkages is critical in climate justice activism. Fossil fuel companies operate and coordinate at the local, national, regional, and international levels, and this means they must be met with countervailing pressure on each of those levels. To do this, climate activists need a wide range of allies—both at home and abroad, with a range of professions and skills. For example, movement allies may include activists from other locales and issue areas; journalists and communications professionals; scientists, engineers, and researchers; certain entrepreneurs and businesses; and attorneys and policymakers with insider connections and institutional access. Ideally, the time to support investment in these linkages and coalitions is *before* a movement needs them, so that they are readily available in times of need.

In particular, **cross-movement linkages between democracy, anti-corruption, and climate justice activists have the potential to be mutually beneficial**. Research finds that a government's willingness to fight climate change depends significantly on that government's level of democracy. For example, according to the Varieties of Democracy Institute (V-Dem), "Moving from the lowest levels of democracy (e.g., China) to the highest (e.g., Canada) equals an increase in policy commitments to climate change mitigation by 19%.... Moving from a fully authoritarian regime to a full democracy... generates a large increase in ambition [targets under the Paris Agreement], equal to almost -1.6°C."[35] Moreover, even among democracies, quality matters. When democracies are corrupt, research finds that they are significantly less likely to implement effective climate policies.[36] Thus, organizers concerned with corruption, democracy, and climate justice organizers have grounds to form common cause.

Supporting such diverse collaboration, and generating significant public support, is increasingly possible as climate change impacts are felt to varying degrees by people all over the world. Each climate disaster is an opportunity for naming the crisis and culprits who profit from it, framing the widely shared experience of insecurity and vulnerability that result from the crisis, and motivating collective response.[37]

Beyond coalition and communications support,

movements also need allies who can help them counter repression. Given the urgency and dire stakes of the climate crisis, climate activism should be seen "as a form of civic engagement" that is welcomed and encouraged among citizens.[38] Yet even in democracies, climate activism has instead come under attack by governments passing repressive laws that infringe upon activists' rights and aim to suppress their ability to mobilize nonviolently to demand action.[39] For example, with support from the oil and gas industry, recent laws in several nominally democratic countries have significantly limited protest locations and vastly increased fines, sentences, and legal liability for nonviolent disruption by climate justice activists.[40] If climate polluters are effective at shutting down people power through repressive laws, it will force people to rely excessively on institutional channels that have already proven inadequate. Thus, fighting repressive laws and defending activists represents a crucial front where movement allies can get involved.

A further opportunity for movement allies is seen in the fact that **climate justice movements are present in countries around the world, but many such movements have received only**

small amounts of support relative to their country's role in global emissions. This is evident in philanthropy, where about "35 percent of climate philanthropy goes to the US and about 10 percent to Europe, which together represent only about 15 percent of future emissions."[41] Meanwhile, several countries that receive comparatively less philanthropic attention but are also major emitters include China, India, Indonesia, South Korea, and Japan. Still other countries may not be large emitters but are critical battlegrounds because they have fossil fuel reserves or territories that are being eyed for pipelines and other infrastructure. These are places where increases in movement support may yield significant decreases in emissions.[42]

Fostering Peace and Security

The Challenge

The year 2022 marked a worsening of global peace and security on several measures. Led by conflicts in Ukraine and Ethiopia, the number of battle-related deaths from interstate and intrastate conflicts rose to their highest level since 1984.[43] 2022 also continued a nearly decade-long high level of "internationalized" intrastate conflicts, in which foreign governments actively support one or more groups of combatants in a civil war.[44] These and other trends are captured in the graph on the following page.[45]

Conflicts among non-state groups (such as criminal or terrorist groups) increased in 2022 as well, which contributed to making it "one of the five most deadly years in non-state conflict since 1989."[46] This is part of a larger trend over the last nine years that has seen "unprecedented levels of

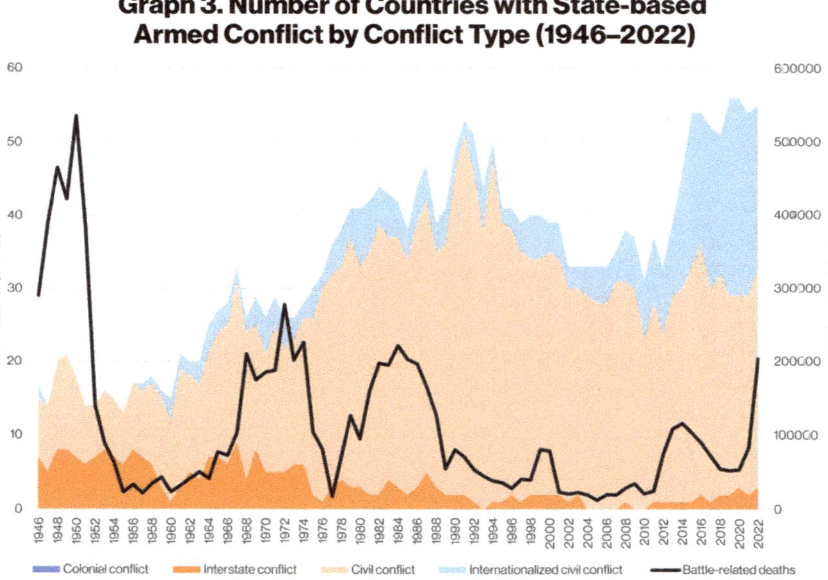

Graph 3. Number of Countries with State-based Armed Conflict by Conflict Type (1946–2022)

Source: Lacina & Gieditsch Battle Death Dataset (2005); UCDP/PRIO Armed Conflict Dataset; UCDP Battle-Related Deaths Dataset (Davies et al., forthcoming) as cited in Júlia Palik, Anna Marie Obermeier, and Siri Aas Rustad, *Conflict Trends: A Global Overview, 1946–2021*, Peace Research Institute Oslo (PRIO), 2022

non-state violence," driven particularly by circumstances in Mexico and Syria."[47]

Amidst this growing violence and insecurity, the impact of conflict on civilians has also increased. According to the Armed Conflict Location and Event Data Project (ACLED), "violence targeting civilians increased by 12% globally in 2022 compared to 2021…. [and] estimated fatalities from direct targeting of civilians grew by at least 16% last year."[48] Political violence also increased by 27 percent over the previous year, with over 125,000 instances recorded in 2022.[49]

The Role of Movements

People power movements can constructively influence conflict, peace, and security in several ways. First, movements can create conditions that reduce the risk of violent conflict and insecurity in societies. Second, movements can reduce a conflict's intensity by shifting the behavior and strategic calculations of armed groups, as well as taking other protective measures toward civilians. Third, people power movements can increase the likelihood that ongoing violent conflicts will reach a peaceful resolution.

Graph 4. Fatalities in Non-state Conflict Between Criminal Gangs Compared to Other Formally Organized Groups (1989–2022)

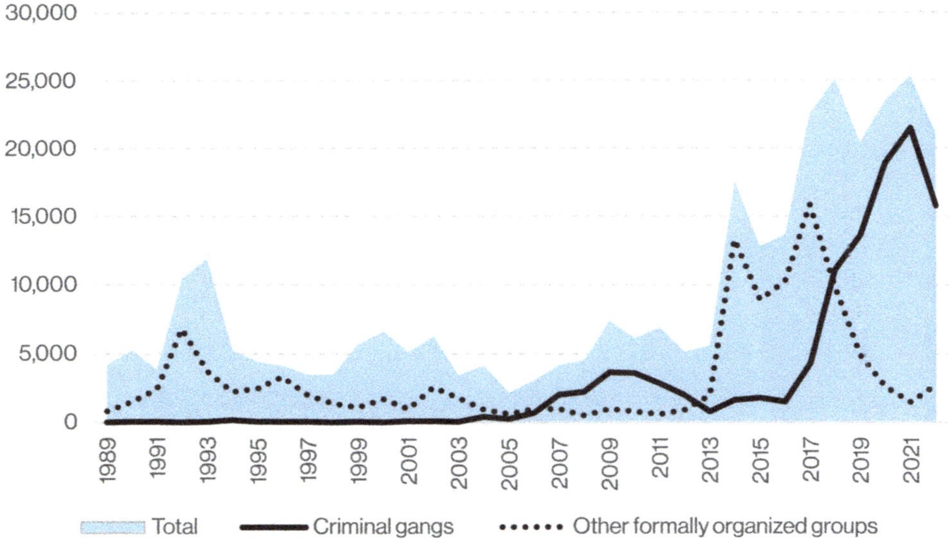

Source: Shawn Davies, Therése Pettersson, and Magnus Öberg, "Organized Violence, 1989–2022, and the Return of Conflict Between States," in *Journal of Peace Research* 60, no. 4 (2023).

To reduce the long-term risk of violent conflict, movements can advance goals—such as democracy, human rights, transparency, and the rule of law—that are conducive to peace and stability. Research shows that democracies are less likely than authoritarian governments to engage in interstate and intrastate wars or to harbor violent non-state actors.[50] As a clear example of this, it is practically unthinkable that a democratic Russia would launch a war against Ukraine, provide military support to the government of Bashar al-Assad in Syria, and harbor the Wagner Group with its international reputation for human rights abuse. This is one stark example of the dangers of a more authoritarian world, but it also points to the potential of people power movements to decrease the risks of violent conflict by fostering democratic transitions.

However, the path from authoritarianism to democracy also contains its own challenges. Periods of democratic transition—whether driven by civil resistance, elite negotiations, or other means—generically result in an increased probability of civil war (as seen in ongoing events in Burma and Sudan).[51] Thus, people power movements with the potential to foster long-term democratic security can also lead to periods of heightened instability. As these movements continue to fight for their rights and democracy, mitigating risks of violence during transitions merits greater attention by the international community.

Another way in which movements can prevent violent conflict is by demonstrating an effective alternative to violence.[52] When communities feel that their fundamental interests are threatened, they are likely to fight by whatever means they think will be strongest. Too often people conclude that joining violent groups is the only viable option, but people power movements can provide a sense of empowerment as well, and redirect people's anger toward engaging in effective nonviolent tactics to address their grievances.[53] This is one possible way to undercut the emergence and recruitment efforts of armed groups.

In ongoing conflicts, armed groups also some-times functionally substitute people power for violence by switching their strategies and tactics (temporarily or more permanently) to nonviolent means.[54] This dynamic has been seen at various points in conflicts in Nepal, East Timor, West Papua, Egypt, South Africa, Palestine, Western Sahara, Mexico, and Colombia.[55]

When a conflict is ongoing, movements can also take actions to decrease its intensity.[56] Research from 16 civil wars in Africa from 1990 to 2009 finds that civilian noncooperation tactics such as strikes and boycotts can significantly reduce conflict deaths.[57] Other studies have found that self-organizing among communities to represent themselves in local talks with armed groups can have similar effects.[58] Cases in Colombia and Syria also suggest that organized civilians in conflict zones may be in a better position than large international organizations (such as the United Nations or the International Committee of the Red Cross) to transmit norms of respect for life and international humanitarian law to armed actors.[59]

Movements can also increase the likelihood that violent conflicts result in a durable and equitable peace. Protests and political engagement by civil society have been effective at driving parties to start peace talks, and disruptive acts such as sit-ins and blockades have been impactful in moving these talks to a peaceful conclusion.[60] More broadly, an analysis of civil wars from 1955 to 2013 finds that when nonviolent movements are active amid armed conflict, the conflict is more likely to result in a negotiated settlement as well as post-conflict democratization.[61] An illustrative example of this is when 5,000 Liberian women from diverse backgrounds organized vigils and protests to drive peace talks in 2003, and then sent a delegation that organized sit-ins and a nonviolent blockade at the negotiation site when peace negotiations seemed to be stalling.[62]

Furthermore, a growing body of scholarship recognizes that direct civil society inclusion in peace negotiations leads to better conflict outcomes. To this end, **acts of nonviolent protest by civil society have been found to increase the probability that civil society groups will be included**—and given substantive roles (such as full participants or mediators)—in peace negotiations.[63]

Lastly, after formal negotiations have ended, **people power movements can play a crucial role in ensuring that all parties live up to their commitments** and that relevant new policies are implemented.[64]

Opportunities and Potential Next Steps

Once violent conflict has commenced in a society, it is notoriously difficult to transition to a sustainable peace. Multifaceted solutions and long-term monitoring and engagement are needed. In line with this, there is a major opportunity to integrate peacebuilding and nonviolent action approaches to addressing conflict. Both fields have similar goals but different emphases (i.e., about taking an impartial or advocacy perspective in a conflict, or about the role of top-down versus bottom-up pressure) and bring a valuable array of tools and insights to this process.[65] Drawing from each of these approaches expands options for practitioners to engage at various stages of a conflict.

In integrating peacebuilding and nonviolent action, the points outlined pertaining to supporting democracy and climate justice movements should be considered, and several further options for movement allies are listed below.

First, **actively reach out to and engage with people power movements at all stages of a conflict—including times of active conflict, during peace negotiations, and during implementation of peace agreements.** Doing this represents a substantive shift, since the traditional mode of trying to resolve violent conflict has often been for armed actors to consume the attention of media and third parties and for civilians to be perceived as powerless victims who need protection. While protecting civilians is critically important, and in some cases civilians have few or no viable options for effective nonviolent action, in other cases a pivotal opportunity is missed by overlooking the agency that civilians have to meaningfully influence the conflict itself.

Even in conflicts where there is no single large movement, but rather several small and highly localized people power movements, they merit engagement. By doing so, peacebuilding actors can expand their repertoire of activities at all stages of their work. In particular, the inclusion of movement representatives during peace negotiations, advocating for their legitimate concerns and aspirations to other actors, and continuing to engage with movements in any post-settlement periods should be seen as baseline for building a lasting peace.

Doing this involves difficult tradeoffs. Armed actors and people power movements often have conflicting demands that may not be reconciled in the short term. Yet over-prioritizing demands of violent actors to the detriment of people power movements in negotiations and post-settlement phases of a conflict (such as happened after the

Sudanese pro-democracy movement ousted autocrat Omar al-Bashir in 2019) can result in unsustainable peace.[66] Failing to address deep power imbalances and issues of structural injustice can pave the way for backsliding.

Second, **movement allies can build their own programs and capacities to support local knowledge sharing, public education, and training efforts on people power.** Among civilian populations facing oppression and injustice, popular demand grows for a need to protect the population and push back against perpetrators of abuse. People power has the potential to out-compete violence in meeting this demand, but investments are needed to share information about its advantages and practical implementation.[67] It is not the role of external actors to lead in this work, but they can support local actors that are concerned about violence and want to advocate for an alternative. Connecting with these people, asking what they need, and offering support—whether funding, information, or introductions to other activists or subject matter experts—can spread public awareness of nonviolent options and empower advocates of people power to make their case.

Third, **support further research on the role of**

people power movements in advancing peace and security. Studies to date point to promising ways that movements can prevent, mitigate, and help resolve violent conflict, and these topics merit further attention. For example, armed conflict often involves highly localized activities by ground forces, and this means that many interactions between nonviolent movements and armed actors are also localized and informal and may not get the visibility they deserve.[68] Therefore, efforts must be made to document, analyze, and share examples and lessons learned from these movements. What strategies are movements using to broker local truces or ceasefires; to enable humanitarian corridors; to create alternative institutions for self-governance and self-reliance; or to organize tactics like protests, strikes, and boycotts that put direct pressure on armed actors? Additional research is also needed on how movements can prevent subsequent relapse of violent conflict after a peace agreement has been reached—are there certain movement strategies, tactics, or options for third-party engagement with movements that shift probabilities on this issue in a constructive direction?

Conclusion

Crises can overwhelm, but they can also focus the mind. They can exacerbate divisions, but they can also forge unity and shared purpose. They can lead to frustration and despair, but they can also lead to bold innovation and creativity. We must choose unity, focus, and innovation—these are the only viable options for a world worth protecting and fighting for.

Progress is possible. Just as a worsening of one crisis can feed the others, so too progress on solving one crisis can help address the others. A first step in doing so is a clear-eyed assessment of what works—and what has not worked—for making change. Strategies can then be adjusted. New capacities can be built. Greater alignment with and support for movements is not the only strategic opportunity in this moment, but it is an essential one that must be taken to fully address a world in peril.

Acknowledgments

This essay was commissioned by ActionAid Denmark (AADK) for the Copenhagen People Power Conference from September 28–29, 2023. I am grateful for their support.

I want to thank and acknowledge those who reviewed drafts and offered specific feedback, including (in alphabetical order): Tom Hastings, Ivan Marovic, Richard Miller, Bruce Pearson, Ines Pousadela, and Tim Whyte. Special thanks to Bruce Pearson also for copyediting and publication production.

About the Author

Hardy Merriman is president of the International Center on Nonviolent Conflict (ICNC) and a nonresident senior fellow at the Atlantic Council's Scowcroft Center for Strategy and Security.

He has worked in the field of civil resistance for over two decades, presenting at workshops for activists and organizers from around the world; developing programs and grantmaking for practitioners and scholars; publishing commentary; and speaking widely about civil resistance movements with academics, journalists, and members of international organizations.

In addition to his leadership of the International Center on Nonviolent Conflict, he also taught as an adjunct lecturer at the Fletcher School of Law and Diplomacy at Tufts University from 2016–2018.

His writings have been translated into numerous languages. Recent publications include *Fostering a Fourth Democratic Wave: A Playbook for Countering the Authoritarian Threat* (2023), *Glossary of Civil Resistance: A Resource for Study and Translation of Key Terms* (2021), and *Preventing Mass Atrocities: From a Responsibility to Protect (RtoP) to a Right to Assist (RtoA) Campaigns of Civil Resistance* (2019).

Endnotes

1. It is difficult to state an exact date at which climate change became a public concern. In 1957 scientists Roger Revelle and Hans Suess commented on CO_2 emissions that "Human beings are now carrying out a large-scale geophysical experiment of a kind that could not have happened in the past nor be reproduced in the future." In 1965 a US President's Advisory Committee panel stated that the greenhouse effect is a matter of "real concern." In 1975 US scientist Wallace Broecker published the article "Climatic Change: Are We on the Brink of a Pronounced Global Warming?" in the journal *Science*, thereby putting the term "climate change" in the public domain.

Sources: Alexandra Witze, "Our Climate Change Crisis," *ScienceNews*, March 10, 2022. https://www.sciencenews.org/century/climate-change-carbon-dioxide-greenhouse-gas-emissions-global-warming#worrisome-predictions-from-climate-models.

"A Brief History of Climate Change," *BBC News*, September 20, 2013. https://www.bbc.com/news/science-environment-15874560.

This Day in History, "The Term 'Global Warming' Appears for the First Time," *History*, August 2, 2022. https://www.history.com/this-day-in-history/global-warming-appears-first-time-paper-science.

2. For example, see: Ville Lähde, "The Polycrisis," *Aeon*, August 17, 2023. https://aeon.co/essays/the-case-for-polycrisis-as-a-keyword-of-our-interconnected-times.

3. Based on definitions in: Bill Moyer, *Doing Democracy* (Gabriola Island, BC: New Society Publishers, 2001).

John McCarthy, "Social Movements," in *Protest, Power, and Change*, edited by Roger S. Powers, William B. Vogele, Christopher Kruegler, and Ronald M. McCarthy (New York: Garland Publishing, 1997).

4. For example, see: Erica Chenoweth and Maria J. Stephan, *Why Civil Resistance Works: The Strategic Logic of Nonviolent Conflict* (New York: Columbia University Press, 2011).

Jonathan Pinckney, *From Dissent to Democracy: The Promise and Perils of Civil Resistance Transitions.* (New York: Oxford University Press, 2020).

5. For review of literature on impacts of climate activism, see: Dana R. Fisher and Sohana Nasrin, "Climate Activism and Its Effects," in *WIREs Climate Change* 12, no. 1 (January/February 2021). https://doi.org/10.1002/wcc.683.

For an example of the impact of people power movements on conflict outcomes, see: Luke Abbs, *The Impact of Nonviolent Resistance on the Peaceful Transformation of Civil War* (Washington: ICNC Press, 2021). https://www.nonviolent-conflict.org/the-impact-of-nonviolent-resistance-on-civil-war-resolution/.

6. For example, see: Hardy Merriman, Patrick Quirk, and Ash Jain, *Fostering a Fourth Democratic Wave: A Playbook for Countering the Authoritarian Threat* (Washington: Atlantic Council, 2023). https://www.atlanticcouncil.org/in-depth-research-reports/report/fostering-a-fourth-democratic-wave-a-playbook-for-countering-the-authoritarian-threat/.

Erica Chenoweth and Maria J. Stephan, *The Role of External Support in Nonviolent Campaigns: Poisoned Chalice or Holy Grail?* (Washington: ICNC Press, 2021). https://www.nonviolent-conflict.org/external-support-for-nonviolent-campaigns/.

7. Freedom House finds 17 years of democratic decline and autocratic resurgence: Yana Gorokhovskaia, Adrian Shahbaz, and

Amy Slipowitz, "Marking 50 Years in the Struggle for Democracy," *Freedom House*, 2023. https://freedomhouse.org/report/freedom -world/2023/marking-50-years/.

V-Dem Insittute finds that "The level of democracy enjoyed by the average global citizen in 2022 is down to 1986 levels." This is calculated by assessing the level of democracy in countries around the world, weighing this level of democracy according to each country's population, and then averaging the results globally. V-Dem Institute, *Democracy Report 2023: Defiance in the Face of Autocratization*, 9–10. https://v-dem.net/publications/democracy -reports/.

8. Some sources on the relationship between authoritarianism and various factors are listed below.

Increasing risk of violent conflict and instability:
V-Dem Institute, *The Case for Democracy: Does Democracy Bring International and Domestic Peace and Security?*, Policy Brief 30, May 11, 2021. https://v-dem.net/media/publications/pb30.pdf.

Insecurity:
V-Dem Institute, *The Case for Democracy: Are Democracies Better for Social Protection of the Poor, Gender Equality, and Social Cohesion?*, Policy Brief 28, May 11, 2021. https://v-dem.net/media /publications/pb_28.pdf.

Humanitarian crises and harboring of violent non-state actors:
Madeleine Albright and Mehdi Jomaa, *Liberal Democracy and the Path to Peace and Security* (Washington: Brookings Institution, September 2017), https://www.brookings.edu/articles/liberal -democracy-and-the-path-to-peace-and-security/.

Corruption:
Clay R. Fuller, *Dismantling the Authoritarian-Corruption Nexus*

(Washington: American Enterprise Institute, July 2019). https://
www.aei.org/wp-content/uploads/2019/07/Dismantling-the
-Authoritarian-Corruption-Nexus.pdf.

Undermining multilateral institutions:

Rana Siu Inboden, *Defending the Global Human Rights System
from Authoritarian Assault: How Democracies Can Retake the Initiative*
(Washington: National Endowment for Democracy, 2023). https://
www.ned.org/defending-the-global-human-rights-system-from
-authoritarian-assault-how-democracies-can-retake-the-initiative/.

Attacks on democracy:

Sharp Power Research Portal: https://sharppower.org/.

9. V-Dem Institute, *The Case for Democracy: Do Democracies
Perform Better Combatting Climate Change?*, Policy Brief 31, May
11, 2021. https://v-dem.net/media/publications/pb_31.pdf.

10. Erica Chenoweth, "The Future of Nonviolent Resistance,"
in *Journal of Democracy* 31, no. 3 (July 2020): 69–84. https://
www.journalofdemocracy.org/articles/the-future-of-nonviolent
-resistance-2/.

11. Chenoweth, "The Future of Nonviolent Resistance."

12. Chenoweth and Stephan, *Why Civil Resistance Works.*

13. Chenoweth and Stephan, *Why Civil Resistance Works.*

14. Judith Stoddard, "How Do Major, Violent and Nonviolent
Opposition Campaigns, Impact Predicted Life Expectancy at
Birth?," in *Stability: International Journal of Security and Develop-
ment* 2, no. 2 (2013). https://doi.org/10.5334/sta.bx.

15. Adrian Karatnycky and Peter Ackerman, *How Freedom is
Won: From Civil Resistance to Durable Democracy* (Washington:
Freedom House, 2005). https://freedomhouse.org/sites/default
/files/How%20Freedom%20is%20Won.pdf

16. Petter Grahl Johnstad, "Nonviolent Democratization:

A Sensitivity Analysis of How Transition Mode and Violence Impact the Durability of Democracy," in *Peace & Change* 35, no. 3 (July 2010). https://doi.org/10.1111/j.1468-0130.2010.00643.x.

17. Merriman, Quirk, and Jain, *Fostering a Fourth Democratic Wave.*

18. See: Chenoweth, "The Future of Nonviolent Resistance." Erica Chenoweth, "Can Nonviolent Resistance Survive COVID-19?," in *Journal of Human Rights* 21, no. 3 (2022): 304–16. doi:2010.1080/14754835.2022.2077085.

19. Chenoweth and Stephan, *The Role of External Support.*

20. Chenoweth and Stephan, *The Role of External Support*, 2.

21. For example, see: Chenoweth and Stephan, *The Role of External Support.*

Benjamin Naimark-Rowse, *Dollars and Dissent: Donor Support for Grassroots Organizing and Nonviolent Movements* (Washington: ICNC Press, 2022). https://www.nonviolent-conflict.org/dollars-and-dissent/.

22. For an example of five movement stages and considerations for external support in each of them, see: Merriman, Quirk, and Jain. *Fostering a Fourth Democratic Wave.*

23. Merriman, Quirk, and Jain. *Fostering a Fourth Democratic Wave.*

24. António Guterres. "Secretary-General Calls on States to Tackle Climate Change 'Time Bomb' through New Solidarity Pact, Acceleration Agenda, at Launch of Intergovernmental Panel Report," *United Nations Press Release*, March 20, 2023. https://press.un.org/en/2023/sgsm21730.doc.htm.

25. *CO2 Emissions in 2022* (Paris: International Energy Agency, March 2023). https://www.iea.org/reports/co2-emissions-in-2022.

26. Oliver Milman, "'Monster Profits' for Energy Giants Reveal a Self-Destructive Fossil Fuel Resurgence," *The Guardian*, February 9, 2023. https://www.theguardian.com/environment/2023/feb/09/profits-energy-fossil-fuel-resurgence-climate-crisis-shell-exxon-bp-chevron-totalenergies.

27. Tara Laan, Anna Geddes, Olivier Bois von Kursk, Natalie

Jones, Kjell Kuehne, Livi Gerbase, Claire O'Manique, Deepak Sharma, and Lorne Stockman, "Fanning the Flames: G20 Provides Record Financial Support for Fossil Fuels," *Energy Policy Tracker*. https://www.energypolicytracker.org/G20-fossil-fuel -support, Accessed September 12, 2023.

28. Impact here can take many forms—for example changing public opinion, driving new policies, changing individual and societal behaviors, and shifting the practices of corporation in ways that reduce greenhouse gas emissions. Fisher and Nasrin, "Climate Activism and Its Effects."

29. John Muñoz, Susan Olzak, and Sarah A. Soule, "Going Green: Environmental Protest, Policy, and CO2 Emissions in U.S. States, 1990–2007," in *Sociological Forum* 33, no. 2 (June 2018): 403–21. https://doi.org/10.1111/socf.12422.

30. H. Christoph Steinhardt and Fengshi Wu, "In the Name of the Public: Environmental Protest and the Changing Landscape of Popular Contention in China," in *The China Journal* 75 (January 2016). https://doi.org/10.1086/684010.

31. Janet K. Swim, Nathaniel Geiger, and Michael L. Lengieza, "Climate Change Marches as Motivators for Bystander Collective Action," in *Frontiers in Communication* 4 (2019). https://doi .org/10.3389/fcomm.2019.00004.

32. Dylan Bugden, "Does Climate Protest Work? Partisanship, Protest, and Sentiment Pools," in *Socius* 6 (2020). https://doi .org/10.1177/2378023120925949.

33. James Ozden, "Protest Movements Could Be More Effective Than the Best Charities," *Stanford Social Innovation Review*, April 14, 2022. https://ssir.org/articles/entry/protest_movements _could_be_more_effective_than_the_best_charities.

GIVINGGREEN.earth, *The Cost-Effectiveness of Donating to Climate Change Activism*, November 2021. https://8741752a-7092-4caf -b230-9daa257c43a3.usrfiles.com/ugd/311d34_3d3357776b424e 4da145fd4c74a3a958.pdf.

34. William Lawrence, "Understanding Sunrise, Part 1: Strategy," *Convergence*, March 14, 2022. https://staging.convergencemag.com/articles/understanding-sunrise-part-1-strategy/.

35. V-Dem Institute, *The Case for Democracy: Do Democracies Perform Better Combatting Climate Change?*

36. Marina Povitkina, "The Limits of Democracy in Tackling Climate Change," in *Environmental Politics* 27, no. 3 (2018): 411–32. https://www.tandfonline.com/doi/epdf/10.1080/09644016.2018.1444723.

37. ASO Communications, "Mobilizing Americans After a Climate Disaster," Rapid Response Memo. https://asocommunications.com/messaging_guides/mobilizing-americans-after-a-climate-disaster/. Accessed September 13, 2023.

38. Fisher and Nasrin, "Climate Activism and Its Effects."

39. International Center for Non-Profit Law and European Center for Non-Profit Law, "Closing Civic Space for Climate Activists," Briefer, June 2020. https://www.icnl.org/wp-content/uploads/Climate-Change-and-Civic-Space-Briefer-vf.pdf.

40. Kristoffer Tigue, "Bold Climate Protests Are Triggering Even Bolder Anti-Protest Laws," *Inside Climate News*, November 22, 2022. https://insideclimatenews.org/news/22112022/bold-climate-protests-are-triggering-even-bolder-anti-protest-laws/.

41. Sigal Samuel, "Want to Fight Climate Change Effectively? Here's Where to Donate Your Money," *Vox*, November 29, 2022. https://www.vox.com/future-perfect/2019/12/2/20976180/climate-change-best-charities-effective-philanthropy.

42. Samuel, "What to Fight Climate Change Effectively?"

43. Anna Marie Obermeier, Håvard Strand, and Georgina Berry, *Trends in State-Based Armed Conflict, 1946–2022, PRIO Conflict Trends*, January 2023. https://cdn.cloud.prio.org/files/1ae379b6-7533-4aba-9b06-13dbbd35adc9/Obermeier%20Strand%20%20Berry%20-%20Trends%20in%20State-Based%20Armed%20Conflict%201946–2022%20-%20Conflict%20Trends%201-2023.pdf.

44. Júlia Palik, Anna Marie Obermeier, and Siri Aas Rustad, *Conflict Trends: A Global Overview, 1946–2021*, Peace Research Institute Oslo (PRIO), 2022. https://cdn.cloud.prio.org/files/988284ec-ec0d-4d9b-ba30-006b223ce98e/Palik%20et%20al%20-%20Conflict%20Trends%20A%20Global%20Overview%20 1946–2021%20PRIO%20Paper%202022.pdf.

45. International non-state actors such as mercenaries (i.e., the Wagner Group) and various terrorist groups are increasingly becoming involved in civil conflicts as well, but the graph on this page only reflects foreign state involvement in civil conflicts.

46. Shawn Davies, Therése Pettersson, and Magnus Öberg, "Organized Violence, 1989–2022, and the Return of Conflict Between States," in *Journal of Peace Research* 60, no. 4 (2023): 691–708. https://doi.org/10.1177/00223433231185169.

47. Davies, Pettersson, and Öberg, "Organized Violence," 695.

48. Timothy Lay, *Global Disorder in 2022: Escalating Violence and the Worsening Civilian Burden*, ACLED, January 2023, 4. https://acleddata.com/acleddatanew/wp-content/uploads/2023/02/ACLED_2022-Year-in-Review_Report_Jan2023.pdf.

49. Lay, *Global Disorder in 2022*.

50. See endnote 8.

51. V-Dem Institute, *The Case for Democracy: Does Democracy Bring International and Domestic Peace and Security?*

52. Hardy Merriman and Jack DuVall, "Dissolving Terrorism at Its Roots," in *Nonviolence: An Alternative for Countering Global Terror(ism)*, edited by Ralph Summy and Senthil Ram (Hauppauge: Nova Science Publishers, 2007). https://www.nonviolent-conflict.org/resource/dissolving-terrorism-at-its-roots-2/.

53. Maria Stephan and Leanne Erdberg, "To Defeat Terrorism, Use People Power," *Minds of the Movement*, March 28, 2018. https://www.nonviolent-conflict.org/blog_post/defeat-terrorism-use-people-power/.

54. Véronique Dudouet, "Dynamics and Factors of Transition

from Armed Struggle to Nonviolent Resistance," in *Journal of Peace Research* 50, no. 3 (2013): 401–13. https://doi.org/10.1177/0022343312469978.

55. Véronique Dudouet, *Civil Resistance and Conflict Transformation Transitions from Armed to Nonviolent Struggle* (New York: Routledge, 2015).

56. Oliver Kaplan, *Resisting War: How Communities Protect Themselves* (Cambridge: Cambridge University Press, 2018).

57. Luke Abbs and Marina G. Petrova, "How—and When—People Power Can Advance Peace Amid Civil War," *United States Institute of Peace*, July 15, 2021. https://www.usip.org/publications/2021/07/how-and-when-people-power-can-advance-peace-amid-civil-war.

58. Oliver Kaplan, "Protecting Civilians in Civil War: The Institution of the ATCC in Colombia," in *Journal of Peace Research* 50, no. 3 (2013): 351–67. https://doi.org/10.1177/0022343313477884.

Juan Masullo Jiménez, *The Power of Staying Put: Nonviolent Resistance Against Armed Groups in Colombia* (Washington: ICNC Press, 2015). https://www.nonviolent-conflict.org/wp-content/uploads/2016/01/The-Power-of-Staying-Put.pdf.

59. Oliver Kaplan, "Nudging Armed Groups: How Civilians Transmit Norms of Protection," in *Stability: International Journal of Security and Development* 2, no. 3 (2013). https://doi.org/10.5334/sta.cw.

60. Abbs and Petrova, "How—and When—People Power Can Advance Peace Amid Civil War."

61. Abbs, *The Impact of Nonviolent Resistance on the Peaceful Transformation of Civil War.*

62. Abbs and Petrova, "How—and When—People Power Can Advance Peace Amid Civil War."

Janel B. Galvanek and James Suah Shilue, *Working Tirelessly for Peace and Equality: Civil Resistance and Peacebuilding in Liberia* (Washington: ICNC Press, 2021). https://www.nonviolent

-conflict.org/wp-content/uploads/2021/05/Working-Tirelessly-for
-Peace-and-Equality-Liberia-SR.pdf.

63. Desirée Nilsson and Isak Svensson, "Pushing the Doors
Open: Nonviolent Action and Inclusion in Peace Negotiations,"
in *Journal of Peace Research* 60, no. 1 (2023): 58–72.
https://doi.org/10.1177/00223433221141468.

64. Véronique Dudouet, *Powering to Peace: Integrated Civil
Resistance and Peacebuilding Strategies* (Washington: ICNC Press,
2017). https://www.nonviolent-conflict.org/wp-content/uploads
/2017/04/powering_to_peace_veronique_dudouet_icnc_special
_report_series_april2017.pdf.

65. Véronique Dudouet, *Powering to Peace.*

66. Sharath Srinivasan, "Support Sudan's Revolution, Not an
Elite Peace Deal," *Foreign Policy*, June 29, 2023. https://foreignpolicy
.com/2023/06/29/sudan-revolution-burhan-hemeti-peace-process/.

67. Merriman and DuVall, "Dissolving Terrorism at Its Roots."

68. Maia Hallward, Juan Masullo, and Cécile Mouly, "Civil
Resistance in Armed Conflict: Leveraging Nonviolent Action to
Navigate War, Oppose Violence and Confront Oppression," in
Journal of Peacebuilding & Development 12, no. 3 (2017): 1–9.
https://doi.org/10.1080/15423166.2017.1376431. This essay has
been slightly modified from its original version.